LIGHTING A CANDLE

LIGHTING A

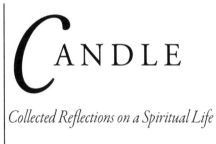

CANDLE

Collected Reflections on a Spiritual Life

COMPILED AND EDITED BY
MOLLY YOUNG BROWN, M.DIV

Lighting A Candle:
Collected Reflections on a Spiritual Life
© 2010 by Molly Young Brown

Psychosynthesis Press,
P.O. Box 1301, Mt Shasta CA 96067
psychosynthesispress.com

First edition published by Hazelden in 1994
Second Edition published by Psychosynthesis Press in 2010
ISBN 978-0-9611444-8-7
Library of Congress Control Number: 2010941030

Cover art by Bernadette Miller.
Technical Editor Ted Slawski
Set in Adobe™ Garamond Premiere Pro

The following authors have given permission to use extended quotations from their copyrighted works: Deena Metzger, "Miracle at Canyon de Chelly"; Mark Morford, untitled essay; Dennis Rivers, excerpt from *Prayer Evolving*.

CONTENTS

Only through directing ourselves toward the moral and the spiritual can we arrive at a state in which life on the earth is no longer threatened by some sort of "megasuicide" and has a genuine human dimension... It is a task that confronts us all, every moment of our existence. We all can and must do something about it; we cannot wait for anyone else.

VACLAV HAVEL

*M*any of us today feel called to the life of the Spirit. We sense that fulfillment and happiness come from awakening to the presence of the divine in our lives. We yearn to celebrate the beauty of life on Earth and to love one another more fully and freely. The rush and complexity of our lives seem to leave no time or energy for spiritual journeying, yet we find ourselves embarked on a spiritual quest, nonetheless.

Our love for the Earth and the children energizes our quest. We know that only greater wisdom and connectedness will help us find solutions to the grave problems facing the world today. Some find support within the religious traditions of their family, while others have explored alternative paths. In either case, most of us seek wisdom from many sources, both within and beyond our religion of origin. We find guidance in the universal truths within all traditions.

The quotations offered here come from a wide array of spiritual traditions, old and new. The women and men quoted are teachers and thinkers from native traditions, Eastern and Western religions, philosophies, spiritual psychologies, and Twelve Step recovery programs. Their words illuminate universal themes of spiritual life for daily inspiration, reflection and meditation.

I have grouped the quotations in four thematic sections, and introduced each with a short reflection. The sections are called:

- Awakening
- Embracing the Darkness
- Love, Grace, and Interbeing
- Action and Service

"Awakening" quotations touch on experiences that first get us started on the spiritual path, experiences that awaken us to the search for meaning and truth. "Embracing the Darkness" contains quotations reflecting the suffering and confusion that sometimes follow our footsteps along the path. "Love, Grace, and Interbeing" quotations illuminate moments when we know we are in the hands of loving forces larger than ourselves, that we are graced by our interconnectedness with earth and universe. "Action and Service" offers quotations to guide us into joyful service in the world.

The order chosen for the sections may or may not follow your personal experience. These movements occur in various sequences for us in different times and circumstances. We may begin in a "dark night of the soul," and then find grace and love through a spontaneous experience of connectedness. Even after many years of spiritual practice and development, we may find ourselves awakening anew to the mystery of it all, or plunging once more into despair and doubt. We learn from all these experiences; they seem to be common to the spiritual journey.

I hope these short epigrams and word poems will speak to you as they have to me, touching secret places, awakening a new understanding, and supporting your struggle and your dance along the way. Although each of us ultimately must find his or her unique spiritual path, I believe we all seek deeper, fuller, committed relationship with every aspect of life on this precious planet.

PART ONE

*A*wakening

What calls us to the spiritual life?
What "divine discontent" awakens us from
ordinary life and ushers us into search and
questioning? Seekers and teachers in many
traditions have spoken of a drive within
us all to awaken to a larger reality and our
relationship to it.

Once awakened, we find ourselves
undertaking a journey of discovery. Our
purpose encompasses wholeness and
balance, centering and understanding, and
deepening our interconnection with all that
is. Teachings may guide us, but ultimately
we must take responsibility for ourselves and
make our own choices. We find that we must
seek within, paying closer attention to our
inner experience, spending time in solitude
and quiet. We begin to surrender to the
mysterious unfolding process of life.

The first group of quotations speak to
this journey of awakening.

At some times in our life a mysterious barrier loosens, and we experience directly that which we have been yearning for or vaguely felt or perhaps just heard about—or never surmised at all. In that incomparable moment the most exquisite, the most prodigious flow of realizations enters our awareness: we have contacted the highest realm of our being.

Piero Ferrucci

A man can live out his entire life without ever finding more than what was already within him as his Beginning Gift, but if he wishes to Grow he must become a Seeker and Seek for himself the other Ways.

Hyemeyohsts Storm

LIGHTING A CANDLE

From the time we are born, there is a wildish urge within us that desires our souls lead our lives, for the ego can only understand just so much.

Clarissa Pinkola Estés

Something has reached out and taken in the beams of my eyes...
All I was doing was being, and the Dancing Energy came by my house.

Mirabai

It may be that when we no longer know what to do, we have come to our real work, and when we no longer know which way to go, we have begun our real journey.

Wendell Berry

People become neurotic when they content themselves with inadequate or wrong answers to the questions of life. They seek position, marriage, reputation, outward success or money, and remain unhappy and neurotic even when they have attained what they were seeking. Such people are usually confined within too narrow a spiritual horizon...If they are enabled to develop more spacious personalities, the neurosis generally disappears.

Carl Jung

Growth is optional. Not all will choose it. Growth means becoming more of who we already are, not what others want us to be. Growth means evolving and waking up, not remaining asleep in the illusions of the learned self.

Brenda Shaeffer

All our lives we have been waiting
for the Mysteries to wake us.
Is the waiting nearly over?
Will the moment overtake us?
Waking hangs on our attention—
that's our greatest Mystery.
When we fully bring attention
to the moment, we will see—
fill the moment with attention—
in that moment we'll be free.

Jim Brown

As long as we are alive we have the power to polish, recut, and place the precious jewel of the self in a brand-new setting.

Earnie Larsen and Carol Larsen Hegarty

The life we want is not merely the one we have chosen and made; it is the one we must be choosing and making. To keep it alive we must be perpetually choosing it and making its differences from among all contrary and alternative possibilities. We must accept the pain and labor of that, or we lose its satisfactions and its joy. Only by risking it, offering it freely to its possibilities, can we keep it.

Wendell Berry

LIGHTING A CANDLE

For me there is only the traveling on paths that have heart, on any path that may have heart. There I travel, and the only worthwhile challenge is to traverse its full length. And there I travel, looking, looking, breathlessly. —Don Juan

Carlos Castaneda

Ultimately there is no way to escape taking responsibility for ourselves.

Tarthang Tulku

Know that, by nature, every creature seeks to become like God...Whether you like it or not, whether you know it or not, secretly nature seeks, hunts, tries to ferret out the track on which God may be found.

Meister Joannes Eckhart

The Sun Dancer believes that each person is a unique Living Medicine Wheel, powerful beyond imagination, that has been limited and placed upon this earth to Touch, Experience, and Learn...
The only way that we can overcome our loneliness is through Touching. It is only in this way that we can learn to be Total Beings. God is a presence of this Total.

Hyemeyohsts Storm

In the beginner's mind there are many possibilities, but in the expert's there are few.

Shunryu Suzuki

You have to be your own teacher and your own disciple. You have to question everything that man has accepted as valuable, as necessary.

Krishnamurti

Finally, you see that there is nothing you can trust—nobody, no authority—except the process itself. Finally the trust is... trusting reality. It is just trust—confidence in the essence itself.

A. H. Almaas

People are not going to find their truth-force or inner authority in listening to the experts, but in listening to themselves, for everyone in her or his way is an expert on what it is like to live on an endangered planet.

Joanna Macy

The problem is...basically: how to remain whole in the midst of the distractions of life; how to remain balanced, no matter what centrifugal forces tend to pull one off center; how to remain strong, no matter what shocks come in at the periphery and tend to crack the hub of the wheel.

Anne Morrow Lindbergh

The basis of the spiritual path is the development in ourselves of what is truly balanced, natural, and meaningful.

Tarthang Tulku

In spiritual practice...the goal is always the recovery of wholeness.

Thomas Matus

There's no place to go; we're always right here. Where could we be except where we are? We always are as we are. Our innate intelligence knows who we are, it knows what we're about in this world if we don't muck it up.

Charlotte Joko Beck

To be completely sensitive to all the implications of life demands that there be no separation between the organism and the psyche. It is a total movement.

Krishnamurti

Breathing in, I calm my body.
Breathing out, I smile.
Dwelling in the present moment
I know this is a wonderful moment.

Thich Nhat Hanh

One's individuality...becomes a gateway for new possibilities and, in its creativity and compassion, becomes a channel for the sacred.

David Spangler

We do, each of us, need to discover our own wholeness. We need to celebrate our personhood.

Karen Casey

Spirituality lets meaning flow into daily life.

David Steindl-Rast

Sincerity is the fulfillment of our own nature, and to arrive at it we need only follow our true self. Sincerity is the beginning and end of existence; without it, nothing can endure. Therefore the mature person values sincerity above all things.

Tzu-ssu

Meditation is to be aware of what is going on—in our bodies, in our feelings, in our minds, and in the world...Life is both dreadful and wonderful. To practice meditation is to be in touch with both aspects. Please do not think we have to be solemn to meditate. In fact, to meditate well, we have to smile a lot.

Thich Nhat Hanh

The witness is always in the here and now and it lives in each instant of living. To be in the witness is to listen with a still heart, with a waiting, open soul, without clinging, without opinions.

Ram Dass

LIGHTING A CANDLE

An attitude of "not-knowing," of opening to the new, can be like rain falling on the hard-packed soil of our lives. If we are willing, it can soften us, so we can feel gratitude and compassion and our own human vulnerability.

Sherry Anderson and Patricia Hopkins

The mature person looks into his own heart and respects what is unseen and unheard. Nothing is more manifest than the hidden; nothing is more obvious than the unseen. Thus the mature person pays attention to what is happening in his inmost self.

Tzu-ssu

Sooner or later we have to learn to let go and allow the changing mystery of life to move through us without our fearing it, without holding or grasping.

Jack Kornfield

Acceptance of the absurd leads to the deepest of all surrenders. Really authentic and full acceptance gives up all comparisons, all expectations, all manipulations. At its core we find gratefulness for the fundamental all-rightness of the universe.

Piero Ferrucci

LIGHTING A CANDLE

I am not, and never have been, the guiding hand in my life. Something—what, I do not venture to say—has prevented what I thought I wanted to do and pushed me into what I eventually did.

Edith Warner

Sometimes life pushes us, and there is usually wisdom in it that we only see later.

Diane Gilman

We are not human beings learning to be spiritual; we are spiritual beings learning to be human.

Jacquelyn Small

Human kindness and compassion, that's my personal religion, maybe it is the universal religion.

The Dalai Lama

PART TWO

*E*mbracing the Darkness

The journey along the spiritual path demands that we face darkness in the world and within ourselves. Old wounds surface, doubts and fears emerge as we venture into the unknown. Yet many spiritual traditions teach that truth may emerge from the darkness, giving us deeper understandings and creative visions.

Today we face not only our personal darkness, but also the pain and despair of a world in crisis. That crisis has come about because of our isolation from nature and from one another, and as we awaken spiritually to our interrelatedness, we experience more deeply the pain of our world.

Spiritual journeying confronts us with our woundedness, our failures and mistakes, our helplessness, hopelessness and need. Yet somehow we may find our way through the darkness by heeding our deepest heart's desire, and by accepting life just as it is.

The next group of quotations illuminate the pain and trials along the spiritual path.

Life is a tragic mystery. We are pierced and driven by laws we only half understand, we find that the lesson we learn again and again is that of accepting heroic helplessness. Some uncomprehended law holds us at a point of contradiction where we have no choice, where we do not like that which we love, where good and bad are inseparable partners impossible to tell apart, and where we—heart-broken and ecstatic—can only resolve the conflict by blindly taking it into our hearts.

Florida Scott-Maxwell

This is not a world for easy.

Roland Merullo

When we are on the verge of making a deep promise, it is not uncommon for great resistances and fears to arise. Whatever threatens our reality or present way of life, whatever we know will profoundly change us, often seems more terrifying than inviting.

Sherry Anderson and Patricia Hopkins

The meeting with oneself is the meeting with one's own shadow. To mix a metaphor, the shadow is a tight pass, a narrow door, whose painful constriction is spared to no one who climbs down into the deep wellspring. But one must learn to know oneself in order to know who one is.

Carl Jung

Doubt, the ruthless hunter,
Lurks within your body;
His arrow has pierced
The flawless diamond of your soul.

Kabir

The movement from certainty to uncertainty is what I call fear...Most of us want to have our minds continually occupied so that we are prevented from seeing ourselves as we actually are. We are afraid to be empty. We are afraid to look at our fears.

Krishnamurti

LIGHTING A CANDLE

Let go of the place that holds, let go of the place that flinches, let go of the place that controls, let go of the place that fears. Just let the ground support me...Walking in the dark night is a way to practice faith, a way to build confidence in the unknown...I learn to practice courage in the vastness of what I can't see...

Stephanie Kaza

We have no reason to distrust our world, for it is not against us. Has it terrors, they are our terrors. If it has an abyss, it is ours. If dangers are there, we must try to love them. And if we would live with faith in the value of what is challenging, then what now appears to us as most alien will become our truest, most trustworthy friend...Perhaps every terror is, in its deepest essence, something that needs our recognition or help.

Rainer Maria Rilke

We have to learn to look at things as they are, painful and overwhelming as that may be, for no healing can begin until we are fully present to our world, until we learn to sustain the gaze.

Joanna Macy

We can never know what strengths and revelations might be on the other side of our fears until we face them and feel them all the way through. True positive thinking is the mental stance of surrender, simply trusting the process. We learn to accept what is.

Jacquelyn Small

Your loving doesn't know its Majesty, until it knows its helplessness.

Rumi

Like all other living things, we must make our descent into the darkness then wait for some new kind of wisdom to take root.

Valerie Andrews

In a dark time the eye begins to see. And this is the paradox: that darkness is the mother of beauty, that the extinction of light is a revelation...Perhaps it is only in the dark times that the pale light of intelligence, going out from the eye, can make its way in the world without being washed away by the fierce light of the sun. Perhaps it is only in the dark times that the eye and the mind, turning to each other, can cooperate in the delicate and impassioned art of seeing.

Chet Raymo

You have hidden the truth in darkness; through this mystery you teach me wisdom.

Psalms 51:6

If only we could see a little farther than our knowledge reaches and a little beyond the borders of our intuition, we might perhaps bear our sorrows more trustingly than we do our joys. For they are the moments when something new enters us, something unknown. Our feelings grow mute in shy embarrassment, they take a step back, a stillness arises, and the new thing, which no one knows, stands in the midst of it all and says nothing.

Rainer Maria Rilke

There are other ways of knowing that are hindered by the light.

Stephanie Kaza

I have been apart and I have lost my way...And in my hours of darkness when I am not even sure there is a Thou hearing my call, I still call to Thee with all my heart. Hear the cry of my voice, clamoring from this desert, for my soul is parched and my heart can barely stand this longing.

Gnostic Holy Eucharist

O Great Spirit, accept my offerings.
O make me understand.

Black Elk

We are pierced and driven by laws we only half understand,
we find that the lesson we learn again and again is that of
accepting heroic helplessness.

Florida Scott-Maxwell

Return to the most human, nothing less
Will teach the angry spirit, the bewildered heart,
The torn mind, to accept the whole of its duress,
And pierced with anguish, at last act for love.

May Sarton

True love and prayer are learned in the hour when love becomes impossible and the heart has turned to stone.

Thomas Merton

Our immediate business, and our quarrel, is with ourselves... We are in danger of losing our souls. We are ignorant of our own nature and confused about what it means to be a human being.

Gary Snyder

How to endure the man-made devastating period in which we live and which seems almost hopeless to control as drought; how to proceed when leadership seems utterly lacking, when individuals and nations seem stupid and arrogant; these are questions no human can answer. I only know that the power recognized by those other sky-scanners still exists, that contact is possible. I know, too, what depths of kindness and selflessness still exist in my fellow-men.

Edith Warner

It is not the desert island nor the stony wilderness that cuts you from the people you love. It is the wilderness in the mind, the desert wastes in the heart through which one wanders lost and a stranger. When one is a stranger to oneself then one is estranged from others too.

Anne Morrow Lindbergh

Our choice is to be in love or to be in fear. But to choose to be in love means to have a mountain inside of you, means to have the heart of the world inside you, means you will feel another's suffering inside your own body and you will weep. You will have no protection from the world's pain because it will be your own.

China Galland

Strength of heart comes from knowing that the pain that we each must bear is part of the greater pain shared by all that lives. It is not just "our" pain but the pain, and realizing this awakens our universal compassion.

Jack Kornfield

It was once thought our fear of earthquakes, our end of the world dreams, our tears at seeing an animal killed by the roadside, were simply projections of our personal anxieties onto our surroundings. Now we are coming to understand that these are also true feelings for Earth itself...The heart of the world beats within each of us and that heart is breaking.

The Book of Sorrow

We suffer with our world—that is the literal meaning of compassion. It isn't some private craziness.

Joanna Macy

Have I known this all my life
and held it buried out of sight?
This aching grief,
this great sadness
for a world gone so far awry?
When it finds its way
through the well-built walls around my heart,
I am frightened and annoyed:
I have no room for this!

Yet feeling this
May be the path to peace.

Molly Brown

Pain comes from experiencing life just as it is, with no
trimmings. We can even call this direct experiencing joy. But
when we try to run away and escape from our experience
of pain, we suffer. Freedom is the willingness to risk being
vulnerable to life.

Charlotte Joko Beck

The truth that many people never understand until it is too late, is that the more you try to avoid suffering the more you suffer.

Thomas Merton

You can hold yourself back from the suffering of the world: this is something you are free to do...but perhaps precisely this holding back is the only suffering you might be able to avoid.

Franz Kafka

Why are you so blind to what the soul needs?
Weep for yourself as when a cloud weeps,
and then the branch freshens. As when a candle
releases tears and gets brighter.

Rumi

The fire of pain traces for my soul
a luminous path across her sorrow.

Rabindranath Tagore

A genuine spiritual path does not avoid difficulties or
mistakes but leads us to the art of making mistakes wakefully,
bringing them to the transformative power of our heart.

Jack Kornfield

He who humbles himself shall be saved.
One who bends shall be made straight.
She who empties herself shall be filled.

Lao Tzu

If we meet God in ourselves, we meet her at the molten core of our heart's desire, ever again energizing our courage and our quest.

Catherine Keller

We all have the same world to respond to. What we practice, we become. If we practice looking at each day as a new adventure, so it will be.

Earnie Larsen and Carol Larsen Hegarty

Stop thinking this is all there is. Realize that for every ongoing war and religious outrage and environmental devastation and bogus Iraqi attack plan, there are a thousand counter-balancing acts of staggering generosity and humanity and art and beauty happening all over the world, right now, on a breathtaking scale, from flower box to cathedral. Resist the temptation to drown in fatalism, to shake your head and sigh and just throw in the karmic towel. Realize that this is the perfect moment to change the energy of the world, to step right up and crank your personal volume; right when it all seems dark and bitter and offensive and acrimonious and conflicted and bilious...there's your opening.

Mark Morford

Out of its abysses, unpredictable life emerges, with a never-ending procession of miracles, crises, healing, and growth. When I realize this once again, I see the absurdity of my belief that I can understand, predict, and control life. All I can really do is go along for the ride, with as much consciousness and love as I can muster in the moment.

Molly Brown

There is one thing in life that you can always rely on: life being as it is.
Life is always going to be the way it is.
Trust in things being as they are is the secret of life.
I can rest in life as it is.

Charlotte Joko Beck

LIGHTING A CANDLE

PART THREE

Love, Grace, and Interbeing

The spiritual path offers joy as well as pain. Mystics and other seekers tell us of experiences of being loved, of being embraced by the universe and graced with its gifts. We come to realize the interconnectedness of all things and our place within the living web of life. Joy, laughter, bliss and beauty fill our hearts.

Love becomes the central force in our lives, opening us to greater understanding and compassion for our brothers and sisters, greater unity with the divine. Our identity widens to embrace all of life around us. We feel a new sense of wholeness and belonging.

The quotations that follow celebrate the love, grace, and "at-one-ment" that many experience along the spiritual path.

One opens the inner doors of one's heart to the infinite silences of the Spirit, out of whose abysses love wells up without fail and gives itself to all.

Thomas Merton

I find there is a quality of being alone that is incredibly precious. Life rushes back into the void, richer, more vivid, fuller than before.

Anne Morrow Lindbergh

What is asked for is a wordless surrender to the divine within you and the acceptance of that grace.

Steven Heckscher

It seems to me that if we approach nature's immensity with the notion that we have a rightful place in it, if we dismiss our puny arrogance and gawky self-consciousness and allow ourselves to be as much an aspect of landscape as any other element, as much a part of the spectrum of life as any other creature—but no more so—then instead of feeling reduced, we might feel exalted at being one among such a magnificent array, at being a jot in the weighty evidence for the creative nature of the universe.

Karen Chamberlain

Willingly, unwillingly
we all melt into God.

Rumi

When you see that God acts through you at every moment,
in every movement of mind or body, you attain true
freedom. When you realize the truth, and cling to nothing in
the world, you enter eternal life.

The Upanishads

And did you get what
you wanted from this life, even so?
I did.
And what did you want?
To call myself beloved, to feel myself
beloved on the earth.

Raymond Carver

God hugs you.
You are encircled by the arms
of the mystery of God.

Hildegard of Bingen

The universe works with you and for you. It is not your enemy.

David Spangler

The world gives itself to us. It gives itself freely to us, if we just allow it. It showers us with gifts.

David Steindl-Rast

This morning I stood on the river bank to pray. I knew then that the ancient ones were wise to pray for peace and beauty and not for specific gifts...And I saw that if one has even a small degree of the ability to take into and unto himself the peace and beauty the gods surround him with, it is not necessary to ask for more.

Edith Warner

Let your awareness drop deep within you like a stone, sinking below the level words can express, to the deep web of relationship that underlies all experience...Out of that vast net you cannot fall. No stupidity, or failure, or cowardice, can ever sever you from that living web. For that is what you are.

Joanna Macy

Grace is the stark knowledge that I am part of the vast, powerful web of life.

Jim Brown

We lie in the lap of immense intelligence, which makes us receivers of its truth and organs of its activities.

R.W. Emerson

There is a larger Mind of which the individual mind is only a sub-system. This larger Mind is comparable to God. But it is immanent in the total interconnected social system and planetary ecology.

Gregory Bateson

The most beautiful experience we can have is the mysterious.

Albert Einstein

The one reality to which we ultimately belong and which therefore most intimately belongs to us can be called God.

David Steindl-Rast

The world and its beings are the spontaneous overflow of creative, imaginative energy.

Huston Smith

The air, blowing everywhere, serves all creatures.

Hildegarde of Bingen

I understood for the first time that love is the very nature
of beauty. I could see the profound tenderness and caring
in the hands of the Maker. It was as if I could feel the heart
from which this beauty emerged; as if the world were not a
separate object, but the embodiment of a love so profound
it absolutely required form; as if the love and form were
not distinct from each other, but different faces of the same
divine presence.
This beauty comes out of great love. This beauty comes out of
a great heart.

Deena Metzger

The universe, by definition, is a single gorgeous celebratory event.

Thomas Berry

Like the grasses showing tender faces to each other, thus should we do, for this was the wish of the Grandfathers of the World.

Black Elk

The fullness of joy is to behold God in everything.

Julian of Norwich

Nothing great was ever achieved without enthusiasm. The way of life is wonderful; it is by abandonment.

R.W. Emerson

Be joyful because it is humanly possible.

Wendell Berry

When the laughter makes people glad they are alive, happy to be here, more conscious of love, heightened with eros, when it lifts their sadness and severs them from anger, that is sacred. When they are made bigger, made better, more generous, more sensitive, that is sacred.

Clarissa Pinkola Estés

The burden of self is lightened
when I laugh at myself.

Rabindranath Tagore

Bliss rises up from within us, not depending on anything
outside...It is the feeling of being awake in the fullness of
each moment.

Jacquelyn Small

Once our hearts are open, all existence appears naturally beautiful and harmonious.

Tarthang Tulku

Love is, in fact, an intensification of life, a completeness, a fullness, a wholeness of life...Love is our true destiny.

Thomas Merton

What permeates the entire being
Like an inexhaustible stream
Alone can be called love.

Kabir

I am in the loving heart of God
wide as the morning sky
I am in the radiant heart of Being
fragrant as a flowering tree
I am in the loving heart of the Universe
shining with endless Light
I am in the infinite heart of God
Whose presence caresses me like a warm wind
I am in the loving heart of Being
which sings through me with angelic voices
I am in the endless heart of the Universe
who holds me like a sleeping child

Dennis Rivers

Truly loving another means letting go of all expectations.
It means full acceptance, even celebration of another's
personhood.
Love is the mortar that holds the human structure together.

Karen Casey

Love your neighbor as yourself.

Leviticus 19:18

Granma said the spirit mind was like any other muscle. If you used it, it got bigger and stronger. She said the only way it could get that way was using it to understand...
Natural, she said, love and understanding was the same thing; except folks went at it backwards too many times, trying to pretend they love things when they didn't understand them. Which can't be done.

Forrest Carter

To develop understanding, you have to practice looking at all living beings with the eyes of compassion. When you understand, you love. And when you love, you naturally act in a way that can relieve the suffering of people.

Thich Nhat Hanh

We each are spinning our individual threads, lending texture, color, pattern, to the "big design" that is serving us all.

Karen Casey

Any true religious practice is to see once again that which is already so: to see the fundamental unity in all things, to see our true face. The main reason we fail to see that which is already so is our fear of being hurt by that which seems separate from us.

Charlotte Joko Beck

Perhaps the most fundamental law is that we are all related.
The universe is not a machine but a harmonious whole.
We have no meaning as isolated entities and can only be
understood in the context of our relationships.

Brenda Shaeffer

Our fulfillment is not in our isolated human grandeur, but
in our intimacy with the larger earth community, for this is
also the larger dimension of our being. Our human destiny is
integral with the destiny of the earth.

Thomas Berry

Who shall define to me an Individual? I behold with awe and delight many illustrations of the One Universal Mind. I see my being imbedded in it. As a plant in the earth so I grow in God. I am only a form of him. He is the soul of me.

R.W. Emerson

I cannot exist without in some sense taking part in you, in the child I once was, in the breeze stirring the down on my arm, in the child starving far away, in the flashing round of the spiral nebula.

Catherine Keller

To see a World in a Grain of Sand
And a Heaven in a Wild Flower
Hold Infinity in the palm of your hand
And Eternity in an hour.

William Blake

What is within us is also without. What is without is also
within. He who sees difference between what is within and
what is without goes evermore from death to death.

The Upanishads

Sacred refers to that which helps take us out of our little selves into the whole mountains-and-rivers mandala universe.

Gary Snyder

There is a Secret One inside us.
The planets in all the galaxies pass through his hands like beads.

Kabir

We are capable of regaining our reverence for life, of replacing the drive to conquer with the will to cooperate. For the first time in our history we can actually see our whole planet and recognize it as a living being—and we can understand that we are not its privileged rulers, as we thought for so long, but only one part, and not even an indispensable part, of its body.

Elizabet Sahtouris

I was seeing in a sacred manner the shapes of all things in the spirit, and the shape of all shapes as they must live together like one being. And I saw that the sacred hoop of my people was one of many hoops that made one circle, wide as daylight and as starlight, and in the center grew one mighty flowering tree to shelter all the children of one mother and one father. And I saw that it was holy.

Black Elk

The spiritual thirst that is latent in everybody can never come to a place of fulfillment unless people begin to think of each other as potential brothers and sisters.

Malidoma Somé

Our determining spirit can be made whole only through the learning of our harmony with all our brothers and sisters, and with all the other spirits of the Universe.

Hyemeyohsts Storm

Heaven is my father and earth is my mother and even such a small creature as I finds an intimate place in its midst. That which extends throughout the universe, I regard as my body and that which directs the universe, I regard as my nature. All people are my brothers and sisters and all things are my companions.

Chang Tsai

The earth is mother of all that is natural,
Mother of all that is human.
She is the mother of all,
for contained in her
are the seeds of all.

Hildegarde of Bingen

My will and my desire were turned by love, the love that moves the sun and the other stars.

Dante

Love is saying yes to belonging.

David Steindl-Rast

PART FOUR

Action and Service

Spiritual teachers tell us that prayer and meditation are not enough. Spiritual journeying requires us to participate in the world, putting our insight and love into action. Fortunately, this is not difficult; the urge to serve seems to flow naturally from our experience of belonging and connectedness.

To truly serve, however, our action must come from careful attention to what is needed, through listening and mindfulness. We learn to act simply and sincerely, while letting go of the results. The world needs us to act with calmness, peace, and involvement, to work together in ways appropriate to our differing gifts. We serve by helping others, and we also serve by celebrating, by "following our bliss."

Because we live within an interconnected web, everything we do matters, everything we do comes back to us along the threads of relationship within our human family and with the living beings who share our planetary home.

Our final group of quotations speak of action and service along the spiritual path.

Action is much more important than simply praying. Unless our insights result in some practical action, they are not useful at all...With compassion, one needs to be engaged, involved.

The Dalai Lama

I slept and dreamt that life was joy. I awoke and saw that life was duty [dharma]. I acted, and behold, duty was joy!

Rabindranath Tagore

Then all at once great happiness overcame me, and it all took hold of me right there. This was to remind me to get to work at once and help bring my people back into the sacred hoop, that they might again walk the red road in a sacred manner pleasing to the Powers of the Universe that are One Power.

Black Elk

Service comes naturally to us when we love and accept ourselves on a deep level. Our love bubbles up and overflows to those around us. We find our greatest satisfaction and fulfillment in making contributions to the world in ways that are uniquely our own. Service is the practice of wholeness.

Molly Brown

When you surrender completely to God, as the only Truth
worth having, you find yourself in the service of all that
exists. It becomes your joy and your recreation. You never tire
of serving others.

Gandhi

When there is no separation between ourselves and others,
naturally we do good. Our basic nature is to do good.

Charlotte Joko Beck

Our possibility is to expand into the world as we experience our own transformation. Many people find this occurs naturally. After all, working on ourselves touches everyone we know. This is inevitable, for we are connected to everything else.

Brenda Shaeffer

Practically speaking, a life that is vowed to simplicity, appropriate boldness, good humor, gratitude, unstinting work and play, and lots of walking brings us close to the actually existing world and its wholeness.

Gary Snyder

Service is the outstanding characteristic of the soul.

Jacquelyn Small

As I open to the love in my heart for my fellow beings—
including the earth—and to my own interdependence and,
indeed, identity with all beings, the yearning to become an
instrument for the relief of all suffering grows stronger.

Ram Dass

Like the sun which emits countless rays, compassion is the source of all inner growth and positive action.

Tarthang Tulku

This "I" which is creating and always giving out something is not the "small I"; it is the "big I." Even though you do not realize the oneness of this "big I" with everything, when you give something you feel good, because at that time you feel at one with what you are giving.

Shunryu Suzuki

There is a sense sometimes of being sustained by something beyond one's own individual power, a sense of being acted "through." One simply finds oneself empowered to act on behalf of other beings—or on behalf of the larger whole—and the empowerment itself seems to come "through" that or those for whose sake one acts.

Joanna Macy

Pain and suffering may often seem to be calling us to jump in and fix things, but perhaps they are asking us first to be still enough to hear what can really help, what can truly get to the cause of this suffering, what will not only eliminate it now but prevent it from returning. So before we act, we need to listen.

Mirabai Bush

Letting others be responsible for themselves is loving and respectful. Letting our friends and loved ones suffer the pain of growth is showing compassion in its purest form.

Karen Casey

Meditating, walking slowly, calming the mind by centering on the breath—these painstaking, deliberate practices increase the odds for acting intelligently in the midst of crisis.

Stephanie Kaza

Return, return to the deep sources, nothing less
Will teach the stiff hands a new way to serve,
To carve into our lives the forms of tenderness
And still that ancient necessary pain preserve.

May Sarton

The truth is that as a man's real power grows and his
knowledge widens, ever the way he can follow grows
narrower: until at last he chooses nothing, but does only and
wholly what he must do.

Ursula LeGuin

In this life we cannot do great things. We can only do small things with great love.

Mother Teresa

My life cannot implement in action the demands of all the people to whom my heart responds.

Anne Morrow Lindbergh

To call the unknown by its right name, "mystery", is to suggest that we had better respect the possibility of a larger, unseen pattern that can be damaged or destroyed and, with it, the smaller patterns. If we are up against mystery, then we dare act only on the most modest assumptions.

Wendell Berry

We do what we do each day, we do it as impeccably as possible, and then we are at peace, realizing that the results are out of our hands.

Ram Dass

We do not have to build a church. Let us be complete in ourselves. Let us drink ourselves empty, give ourselves fully, extend ourselves outward—until, at last, the waving treetops are our own gestures and our laughter is resurrected in the children who play beneath them...

Rainer Maria Rilke

All I can do is engage with complete sincerity. Then, whatever happens, there is no regret.

The Dalai Lama

Ancient Ones,
residing in this forest,
speak to me.
Fill me with your wildness,
your wisdom,
your abiding Now.
Let me see all the projects and tasks
that consume my days
in the vast perspective of your time.
Let me see them as at one with
the forming of a seed cone,
the pushing out of leaf and stem
the chatter of grey squirrel
the flight of chickadee
the flow of water in the creek:
All taking place within the embrace of Life;
All held in love.

Molly Brown

I understood that work was another way of worshipping,
that listening and working were one and the same thing.

Beautiful Painted Arrow

The object of work is to cultivate mindfulness and complete absorption. All labor entered into with such a mind is valued for itself apart from what it may lead to. All work is ennobling, because it is seen as an expression of Buddha-nature. This is true enlightenment and enlightenment is never for oneself alone but for the sake of all.

Roshi Philip Kapleau

Work alone is your privilege, never the fruits thereof. Never let the fruits of action be your motive; and never cease to work. Work in the name of God, abandoning all selfish desires. Be not affected by success or failure.

The Bahgavad Gita

We need people who can sit still and be able to smile, who can walk peacefully. We need people like that in order to save us. Buddhism says that you are that person, that each of you is that person.

Thich Nhat Hahn

What we want to do
is become like Jesus
—to have that still center
that nothing can disturb.
In that way
we are true peacemakers,
persons who project peace
wherever we go.

Mary Lou Kownacki

Real activity is combined with calmness which can't be ruffled. It is a balance of mind which is never disturbed whatever happens. Only when the mind is calm and collected is the whole of its energy spent in doing good work.

Swami Vivekenanda

I pray that I may have the courage to help bring about what the weary world needs but does not know how to get.

Twenty-four Hours a Day

You just do whatever you do to serve in a way that increases the connection of humanity, the awareness of the interrelatedness of all things. You are more effective and efficient in any action when you are capable of being totally involved in what you're doing, and totally non-attached.

Ram Dass

We are realizing that in an interconnected world, not only are problems interwoven, but the solutions are interconnected as well, which means whatever we do to help ourselves and our world, we must do it together.

David Spangler

Grace happens when we act with others on behalf of our world.

Joanna Macy

In today's highly interdependent world, individuals and nations can no longer resolve many of their problems by themselves. We need one another. We must therefore develop a sense of universal responsibility...It is our collective and individual responsibility to protect and nurture the global family, to support its weaker members, and to preserve and tend to the environment in which we all live.

The Dalai Lama

In planetary service, all work and workers are equal...All Service leads to the good of the whole.

Jacquelyn Small

If you want to raise a man from mud and filth, do not think it is enough to keep standing on top and reaching down to him a helping hand. You must go all the way down yourself, down into mud and filth. Then take hold of him with strong hands and pull him and yourself out into the light.

Rabbi Shelomo

What we do anywhere matters...It matters very much. Mesas and mountains, rivers and trees, winds and rains are as sensitive to the actions and thoughts of humans as we are to their forces. They take into themselves what we give off and give it out again.

Edith Warner

Humankind is called to co-create. With nature's help, humankind can set into creation all that is necessary and life-sustaining.

Hildegard of Bingen

He who celebrates is not powerless. He becomes a creator because he is a lover.

Thomas Merton

If we are here for any good purpose at all...I suspect it is to entertain the rest of nature. A gang of sexy primate clowns. All the little critters creep in close to listen when human beings are in a good mood and willing to play some tunes.

Gary Snyder

Practice random kindness and senseless acts of beauty.

Anne Herbert

Let the beauty we love be what we do.
There are hundreds of ways to kneel and kiss the ground.

Rumi

LIGHTING A CANDLE

BIBLIOGRAPHY

Almaas, A. H.
    Diamond Heart, Book One, Berkeley: Diamond
    Books, 1987.
Anderson, Sherry, and Patricia Hopkins
    The Feminine Face of God, New York: Bantam, 1991.
Andrews, Valerie
    A Passion for This Earth, San Francisco: Harper &
    Row, 1990.

Bateson, Gregory
    Steps to an Ecology of Mind, New York: Ballentine,
    1972.
Beautiful Painted Arrow. See Rael, Josepth.
Beck, Charlotte Joko
    Everyday Zen, San Francisco: HarperSanFrancisco,
    1989.
Berry, Thomas
    The Dream of the Earth, San Francisco: Sierra Club
    Books, 1988.
Berry, Wendell
    A Continuous Harmony, New York: Harcourt, Brace
    & Jovanovich, 1972.
    The Gift of Good Land, San Francisco: North Point,
    1983.
    Home Economics, San Francisco: North Point, 1987.
Black Elk.See Neihardt, John.
Blake, William
    "To See the World in a Grain of Sand" in *A
    Continuous Harmony*, by Wendell Berry. New York:
    Harcourt, Brace & Jovanovich, 1972.

The Book of Sorrow
>In The Box. Santa Fe, NM: The Térma Company, 1992.

Brown, Jim
>"Any Moment," unpublished poem.
>"Grace" in unpublished journal.
>Personal communication.

Brown, Molly
>*Growing Whole*, Mt Shasta CA: Psychosynthesis Press, 2009.
>"Forest Prayer," unpublished poem.
>"Path to Peace," unpublished poem.

Capra, Fritjof, and David Steindl-Rast
>*Belonging to the Universe*, HarperSanFrancisco, 1991.

Carter, Forrest
>*The Education of Little Tree*, Albuquerque: UNM Press, 1976.

Carver, Raymond
>"Late Fragment," *A New Path to the Waterfall*, The Atlantic Monthly Press

Casey, Karen
>*Each Day a New Beginning*, Center City MN: Hazelden, 1991.

Castaneda, Carlos
>*The Teachings of Don Juan*, Berkeley: UC Press, 1968.

Chamberlain, Karen
>*Desert of the Heart*, Denver CO: Ghost Road Press, 2006.

Chang Tsai
> *In A Dream of the Earth*, by Thomas Berry. San
> Francisco: Sierra Club Books, 1988.

The Dalai Lama
> *A Policy of Kindness*, Ithica NY: Snow Lion, 1990.
> *Worlds in Harmony*, Berkeley: Parallax, 1992.
> In *Longing for Darkness*, by China Galland. New
> York: Penguin, 1990.

Dante
> *The Divine Comedy*, In C. E. Norton translation,
> "Great Books" series, Encyclopedia Britannica,
> 1952.

Eckhart, Meister
> *Meister Eckhart*, Translated by R. Blakney. New
> York: Harper & Row, 1941.

Einstein, Albert
> *Ideas and Opinions*, New York: Bonanza Books,
> 1954.

Emerson, Ralph Waldo
> "Self-Reliance" & "Circles." In *Selections from
> Ralph Waldo Emerson*, Edited by Stephen Whicher.
> Cambridge: Riverside, 1957.

Estés, Clarissa Pinkola
> *Women Who Run with the Wolves*, New York:
> Ballantine, 1992.

Ferrucci, Piero
> *What We May Be*, Los Angeles: J. P. Tarcher, 1982.

Fox, Matthew
> *Original Blessing*, Santa Fe NM: Bear & Company,
> 1983.

Galland, China
> *Longing for Darkness*, New York: Penguin, 1990.

Gandhi, Mahatma
> *The Words of Gandhi*, Edited by R. Attenborough.
> New York: Newmarket, 1982.

Gilman, Diane
> Personal communication, 1993.

Havel, Vaclav
> *Disturbing the Peace*, New York: HarperCollins,
> 1990.

Heckscher, Steven of St. Gregory's Abbey
> In class reader compiled by Ana Matt, Graduate
> Theological Union, Berkeley CA, 1992.

Herbert, Anne, and Margaret M. Pavel
> *Random Kindness and Senseless Acts of Beauty*,
> Volcano, CA: Volcano, 1993.

Hildegard of Bingen
> In *Original Blessing*, by Matthew Fox. Santa Fe,
> NM: Bear & Company, 1983.

Julian of Norwich
> In *Original Blessing*, by Matthew Fox. Santa Fe,
> NM: Bear & Company, 1983.

Jung, Carl
> *Memories, Dreams, Reflections*. New York: Vintage/
> Random House, 1965.
> "The Integration of the Personality." In *The Choice is
> Always Ours*. Translated by .S. Dell. Edited by D. B.
> Phillips, E. B. Howes & L. M. Nixon. San Francisco:
> Harper & Row, 1975.

Kabir

> *The Weaver of God's Name.* Edited by V. K. Seithi.
> Punjab, India: Radha Soami Satsang Beas, 1984.
> In *World as Lover, World as Self,* by Joanna Macy.
> Berkeley: Parallax, 1991.

Kafka, Franz

> In *World as Lover, World as Self,* by Joanna Macy.
> Berkeley: Parallax, 1991.

Kapleau, Roshi Philip

> *The Three Pillars of Zen*, Garden City, NY: Anchor
> Press, 1980.

Kaza, Stephanie

> *The Attentive Heart*, New York: Ballantine, NY,
> 1993.

Keller, Catherine

> From a *Broken Web*, Boston: Beacon, 1986.

Kownacki, Mary Lou

> *PeaceMaking Day by Day 1*, Erie, PA: Pax Christi
> USA.

Kornfield, Jack

> *A Path With Heart*, New York: Bantam, 1993.

Krishnamurti, J.

> *Freedom from the Known*, New York: Harper &
> Row, 1969.

Larsen, Earnie, and Carol Larsen Hegarty

> *Days of Healing, Days of Joy*, Center City MN:
> Hazelden, 1987.

Lao Tzu

> *Tao Teh Ching*, Adapted from verse 22, based on
> traditional translations.

LeGuin, Ursula
>*Wizard of Earthsea*, New York: Atheneum/
>Macmillan, 1968.

Lindbergh, Anne Morrow
>*Gift from the Sea*. New York: Vintage/Random
>House, 1975.

Macy, Joanna
>*World as Lover, World as Self.* Berkeley: Parallax,
>1991.

Mirabai
>In *Mirabai Versions* by Robert Bly. New York: The
>Red Ozier Press, 1980.

Matus, Thomas
>In *Belonging to the Universe*, by Fritjof Capra,
>and David Steindl-Rast. San Francisco: Harper
>SanFrancisco, 1991.

Merton, Thomas
>*Love and Living*, Edited by N. B. Stone and P. Hart.
>New York: Bantam, 1979.
>In *A Path with Heart*, by Jack Kornfield. New York:
>Bantam, 1993.

Metzger, Deena
>"Miracle at Canyon de Chelly." In *The Sun*, No. 146,
>January 1988.

Miller, R
>"The Gnostic Holy Eucharist Service." In *Seeing
>Through the Visible World*, by June Singer.
>HarperSanFrancisco, 1990.

Morford, Mark
>Excerpt appearing in *Sun Magazine*, March 2003.

Mother Teresa
>In *A Path with Heart*, by Jack Kornfield. New York:
>Bantam, 1993.

Merullo, Roland
>*Breakfast with Buddha*, Chapel Hill NC: Algonquin
>Books of Chapel Hill, 2007.

Neihardt, John (as told through)
>*Black Elk Speaks,* Lincoln NE: UN Press, 1979.

Nhat Hanh, Thich
>*Being Peace*, Berkeley: Parallax, 1987.

Prabhavananda, Swami and Christopher Isherwood, trans
>*The Song of God: Bhagavad Gita*, New York: New
>American Library, 1954.

Prabhavananda, Swami and Frederick Manchester, trans
>*The Upanishads: Breath of the Eternal*, New York:
>New American Library, 1948.

Rael, Joseph E
>*Beautiful Painted Arrow*, Rockport, MA: Element,
>Inc. 1992.

Ram Dass
>In class reader (from a lecture sponsored by Seva
>Foundation, at St. John the Divine Church, New
>York City). Compiled by Ana Matt, Graduate
>Theological Union, Berkeley, CA, 1992.

Ram Dass & Mirabai Bush
>*Compassion in Action*, New York: Bell Tower, 1992.

Raymo, Chet
>*The Soul of the Night*, New York: Prentice Hall,
>1985.

Rilke, Rainer Maria
    "Letters to a Young Poet" and "Early Journals." In A
    Year with Rilke, Joanna Macy and Anita Barrows,
    translators and editors, New York: Harper Collins,
    2009.
Rivers, Dennis
    Prayer Evolving, Berkeley CA: Karuna Books, 2008.
Rumi, Jalaluddin
    Feeling the Shoulder of the Lion, Translated by
    Coleman Barks. Putney, VT: Threshold Books,
    1991.
    Open Secret, Translated by John Moyne and
    Coleman Barks. Putney, VT: Threshold Books,
    1984.
    This Longing, Translated by Coleman Barks.
    Threshold Books, Putney, VT, 1984.
    Fragments, Ecstacies, Translated by Daniel Liebert.
    Cedar Hills, MO: Source Books, 1981.

Sahtouris, Elizabeth
    Gaia-The Human Journey from Chaos to Cosmos,
    New York: Pocket Books, 1989.
Sarton, May
    "Santos, New Mexico" in *The Lion and the Rose*,
    New York: Rinehart, 1948.
Scott-Maxwell, Florida
    The Measure of My Days, New York: Alfred A.
    Knopf, 1968.
Shaeffer, Brenda
    Loving Me, Loving You, Center City MN:
    Hazelden, 1991.

Shelomo, Rabbi
>In Tales of the Hasidim–Early Masters, by Martin
>Buber. New York: Random House, 1961.

Small, Jacquelyn
>Awakening in Time, New York: Bantam, 1991.

Smith, Huston
>The World's Religions, San Francisco:
>HarperSanFrancisco, 1991.

Snyder, Gary
>The Practice of the Wild, San Francisco: North Point,
>1990.

Somé, Malidoma
>Interview In Context #34 (Winter 93).

Spangler, David
>Conversations with John, Elgin, IL: Lorian Press,
>1980.
>Interview, In Context #34 (Winter, 1993).

Steindl-Rast, David, and Fritjof Capra
>Belonging to the Universe, San Francisco:
>HarperSanFrancisco, 1991.

Storm, Hyemeyohsts
>Seven Arrows, New York: Ballantine, 1972.

Suzuki, Shunryu
>Zen Mind, Beginner's Mind, New York: Weatherhill,
>1970.

Tagore, Rabindranath
>Fireflies, New York: Collier/MacMillan, 1928,
>1955.

Tsai, Chang
>In Dream of the Earth, by Thomas Berry. San
>Francisco: Sierra Club Books, 1988.

Tulku, Tarthang
    Gesture of Balance, Emeryville CA: Dharma
    Publishing, 1977.
Twenty-four Hours a Day
    Center City, MN: Hazelden, 1975
Tzu-ssu
    *In The Enlightened Mind: An Anthology of Sacred
    Prose*, Edited by Stephen Mitchell. New York:
    HarperPerennial, 1989.

The Upanishads
    *In The Enlightened Mind: An Anthology of Sacred
    Prose*, Edited by Stephen Mitchell. New York:
    HarperPerennial, 1989.

Vivekananda, Swami
    In course reader compiled by Ana Matt, Graduate
    Theological Union, Berkeley CA, 1992.

Warner, Edith
    In The House at Ottowi Bridge, by Peggy P. Church
    Albuquerque: University of New Mexico Press,
    1960.

Index of First Lines